The JOY and ADVENTURE of GROWING YOUNGER

by Mary Kimbrough

Publishing House
St. Louis

To **one** who would not retreat, who possess-
ed the spirit to adventure, the eyes to see, the
hunger to learn, the heart to love, and the faith
to take the wings of the morning,
To **all** who laugh at the years and grow a
little younger every day,
This book is dedicated, with love.

Copyright ©1983 by Concordia Publishing House
3558 South Jefferson Avenue
St. Louis, MO 63118

Printed in the United States of America

Library of Congress Cataloging in Publication Data

Kimbrough, Mary.
  The joy and adventure of growing younger.

  1. Retirement—United States. 2. Aged—United States—Religious
life. I. Title.
HQ1064.U5K476   1983   646.7'9   82-14409
ISBN 0-570-03875-8 (pbk.)

Contents

Chapter 1

How to Grow Young — and Like It

If I take the wings of the morning and dwell in the uttermost parts of the sea, even there shall Thy hand lead me, and Thy right hand shall hold me.

Psalm 139:9-10

Retirement is a time of decision.

Where will you live? Will you work part time? What hobbies will you pursue? Will you go back to school?

But an even more important choice awaits you. It's your decision to make. No one can make it for you.

Which will you choose — fear? or freedom and fun?

How will you live — in fear? or with faith?

No one has promised humankind a rose garden without thorns or years without tears. No one has guaranteed that sorrow can be wiped away with a smile. But a stalwart faith in God's goodness can dull the sharp pain of the thorns and ease the ache of grief.

Fear thou not; for I am with thee; be not dismayed; for I am thy God. I will strengthen thee; yea, I will help thee; yea, I will uphold thee with the right hand of MY righteousness.

Isaiah 41:10

Retirement is a special time — a time to take the wings of the morning, to sing a new song, to walk an uncharted road.

Retirees are a special company — not a

vanishing breed. More than 1 American in 10 is 65 or older, and by the year 2,000, scientists predict, that ratio will be 1 in 5. The youth-oriented society will disappear. The future belongs to the older adult.

It's your future. Your world. Your choice. It can be a drab time, as gray as a cloud-filled sky on a January morning. Or it can be a shining time, as lovely as an April afternoon.

This book is designed to help you make your choice. It is dedicated to the still-active, to the quieter ones, and to those who, although shut in, refuse to be shut out.

May you find in its pages a little fun, a little adventure, and a small challenge to live life with zest and joy. Retirement is not to be confused with life's passage from maturity to old age, no matter what the calendar and your social security card say. It is not the accepted time — unless you want it to be — for sliding downhill and slipping into oblivion.

Retirement can be far more than a gold watch, a farewell salute, an office party and, then, a sudden stab of panic. Retirement need not mean too many yesterdays and too few tomorrows, a string of empty hours woven into dingy days of nowhere to go, nothing to do, no new horizons to view, no new races to be run, no new dreams to be dreamed.

Retirement is stepping out of the pressurized cabin of alarm clocks, three-week vacations, profit-and-loss sheets, office memos, and time slips into the fresh, tangy air of a wondrous world of labor, learning, and leisure.

Retirement is exchanging the responsibilities of parenthood for the joys of grandparenthood.

Retirement is trading the burdens of the marketplace for the lighter load of a less-structured day.

Retirement is adventure. It's the door newly opened, the pathway newly taken. It's the mountain to be climbed, the small risk to be dared, the far reaches of the mind and spirit to be explored.

Retirement, more than all else, is time — not time to be killed, but time to be lived. Time to know the blessing of dawn's newness, the sundrenched glory of noontide, the healing quiet of evening, the eternal peace of the starlit night.

Retirement is time for friendship and laughter, time for savoring the familiar and the cherished, time for discovery.

Retirement is time for giving and trusting, living and loving, believing and preparing.

Fear or freedom?

Fear or faith?

The pioneer made that choice and built a strong America. Your ancestors made that choice and, against far more devastating odds than are thus far faced by this generation, planted their roots in the soil of a new land.

The wrinkles and the slower step may fool you into thinking that you have reached the age of weariness and discontent, the worst of times, the end of the road.

All you need to be weary of is sitting down and watching the world pass you by.

Your only discontent should be with the stereotypes and the status quo.

For you, the "worst of times" can be the "best of times."

For you, the end of the road may be the beginning of another.

So take the wings of the morning into retirement. Sing a new song. Walk an uncharted road.

Retirement is your special time.

Thou shalt be steadfast, and shalt not fear; ...thine age shall be clearer than the noonday; thou shalt shine forth, thou shalt be as the morning.

Job 11:15, 17

Retirement is a time to recycle life's sameness and to dare the seemingly impossible.

Retirement is a time to grow. It is a time to stretch the mind, to spark the spirit, to feed the heart's hungers, and to nourish faith. It is a time to watch, without fear, as one chapter ends and to wait, without doubt, as another begins.

Retirement is a special time.

It can be the time of your life.

It can be the prime of your life.

Chapter 2
Fun Is the Name of the Game

You have been out to dinner with friends. It's your turn to be host and hostess, and now everyone has come back to your home to finish the evening with dessert and games. You're bored with bridge and bingo. No one likes canasta or pinochle. You haven't gone dancing since your 10th wedding anniversary.

★   ★   ★

You're the social director for a retirement or nursing home. A group of residents, even those who get around with walkers or wheelchairs, has gathered in the rec room. The TV die-hards have huddled in the corner with their favorite program, but for many, canned entertainment is as stimulating as a wet dishrag.

What's your E.Q. — your "entertainment quotient?"

How can you make sure that your guests will have a good time?

They may be active or sedentary, jolly or solemn, learned or with little formal education.

But they all are retirees, seniors, or shut-ins. If you ask them what party entertainment they enjoyed in the B.T. (before television) era, you probably will hear one answer above all others: parlor games.

The name "parlor games" itself is clothed with nostalgia, for these games were born of a simpler, gentler life-style than we know today. To play them again may not recapture one's youth, but they will conjure up memories of the

11

happiest evenings of a generation or two ago.

Here are some of those old-fashioned parlor games. They may need to be adapted to the age and physical abilities and special interests of the players. Some have changed through the years. But all will be remembered.

Charades

A charade is make-believe. It's like an old-fashioned silent movie. It's a bit of Broadway in your own living room. You can even award an "Oscar" for the best performance.

The rules of charades have many variations, but these are basic:

1. Choose up sides or divide the group into two.

2. The side which is "it" can either select a slip of paper that the leader has prepared in advance, or players can get together to decide what they will act out.

3. The "act" can be the title of a song, book, play, movie, painting, or it can merely be a multisyllable word. Don't select something that can be easily guessed after the first syllable or word.

4. A captain relays the hints to the other side, and either two or three selected actors or the entire group can act out the word or words.

5. Agree in advance how hints are to be given. One popular way is to use certain gestures to identify the mystery as a book, play, song, or whatever. Then the captain begins to give additional hints. He or she holds up fingers to indicate the number of words. Let's say the mystery is the painting, "Washington Crossing the Delaware." The leader indicates that this is a painting of four words, then holds up one finger to show that the team will now act out the **first word.** He can point to the first knuckle to indicate this is the **first syllable** of the

word. "Wash," of course, could be indicated by pretending to use a scrub board. "Ton" could be shown by pretending to carry something extremely heavy.

When the first word, "Washington," has been guessed, the captain will indicate that his team will act out the **second word.** Everyone on the team can frown until the other team guesses "cross."

"Delaware" could be broken down into syllables, but unless the guessing team is familiar with such names as "Della" Street and "Della" Reese — which could be acted out — the captain may have to start with "ware," indicating that this is the **last syllable.** This could be acted out as though it were spelled "wear." (Don't worry about sound-alike words spelled differently. That just adds to the befuddlement of the opposing team and the fun of the game).

Proverb Pantomime

This is a version of the basic charades game. One side agrees on a proverb to act out. It can be from the Bible or can be a well-known saying. The group then acts out in pantomime the quotation, while the other side tries to guess. Time each group of guessers and at the end of the game give silly prizes to members of the winning side.

By using unfamiliar axioms or proverbs, the game can be made extremely challenging and difficult. Your particular group may respond better to sayings that are easier to guess.

Here are some suggestions:

"A man's pride shall bring him low; but honor shall uphold the humble in spirit" (Prov. 29:23).

"Speak not in the ears of a fool, for he will despise the wisdom of thy words" (Prov. 23:9).

"She is not afraid of the snow for her household; for all her household are clothed with scarlet" (Prov. 31:21).

"Make hay while the sun shines."

"It's the shovel that laughs at the poker."

"All's well that ends well."

"Don't give up the ship."

BIBLICAL CHARACTERS

Divide into two groups. One selects a Biblical character, and members of the other team ask questions that can be answered only by yes or no. It's a name version of the old "What's My Line?" television show.

Don't choose the obvious ones — Paul or Matthew or Abraham or Ruth. Select those who are not so well-known except, of course, to serious Bible students.

The questions might be:

"Is it a man?"

"Is he or she in the Old Testament?"

"Was she a widow?"

"Did this person meet a violent death?"

"By stoning?"

"Did he build a magnificent temple?"

"Did he get the world's most famous haircut?"

Pride and Prejudice

No one is as proud — or as prejudiced — as a grandparent. Ask your guests to bring unidentified snapshots of their grandchildren and put them on display. Let all the guests guess who belongs to whom.

To add spice to the game, ask each guest to bring a picture of himself or herself. If possible, that should be a baby picture. Then let the guests try to match the faces.

Possible prizes: a $5 gift certificate to be

spent for the grandchild, with a card containing a Polaroid snapshot of all the guests at the party; an appealing commercial print of a baby; a $5 bill to be spent on a telephone call to an out-of-town grandchild; a mint set of coins for this particular year, or a shiny new dime with the year of the child's birth.

If you are a social director in a home, consider setting aside a Grand (for "grandparents") Room where grandchildren's snapshots can be displayed. This could be permanent, building over the years, or it could be changed periodically to display "the grandchild of the month." The latter would require some hard and fast rules — or a name-drawing — so that no one would be hurt if his or her relative were not chosen.

What's in a Name?

This is a difficult contest requiring a great deal of imagination, but it can be fun. It challenges guests to think of an individual in other than mere physical (height, coloring, etc.) terms.

First, agree on a category. It could be automobiles or furniture or television programs or kitchen equipment or tourist attractions. Now, divide into teams. The object is to describe a certain individual in terms of that category.

For example, if the category is automobiles, a thrown-together, unkempt teenager might be described as a "pickup truck with dented fenders," while a petite grandmother might be "an electric car with a tea rose in the bud vase." (Remember those?)

Or if the category is furniture, a rugged man might be an oak desk: a precise, slightly old-fashioned individual might be a rolltop desk, and a delicate, beautifully groomed person might be a Queen Anne chair or French provincial dressing table.

16

The person being described could be one of the party or it could be a famous person. The latter probably is wiser, as feelings can be easily hurt even by a well-intentioned joke. Each member of the "it" team can give his or her description until one of the opposing team guesses the identity.

Red, White, and Blue Magic

This is a mystery game in which the leader must have an accomplice who is said to be "psychic" and "able to read our minds." The accomplice leaves the room and an object is selected. The leader then asks the questions.

"Is it that table?" "No."

"Is it that clock?" "No."

"Is it the third book from the left on the shelf?" "No."

"Is it the heel of Mrs. Smith's right shoe?" "Yes."

The secret clue is the book, which has a **red** binding. The accomplice knows that the **next** clue will be the right one.

The "gifted" accomplice goes out again. This time, the mystery clue is changed to **white.** A white object is mentioned just before the correct one. The third time, a **blue** object will be the key. It will be some time before the guests figure out how the so-called "mind reader" performs so successfully.

Mystery Ashes

The leader holds enough slips of paper for each person in the group. He or she asks each guest to name a famous person, then writes a name on the slip, folds it and places it in a bowl. The slips are shuffled and one guest is asked to draw one but to keep it folded.

Now the leader places the remaining slips

in an ash tray and burns them — promising to find from the ashes the identity of the person whose name is on that one slip held by the guest. The leader pretends to study the ashes and, at last, announces the name. The guest opens the slip and, lo and behold, the announced name is indeed there.

How is it done?

Simple. The leader has written the **same** name on every slip. No one knows this, because the others have been burned. Of course, the slip held by the guest will bear the name so "magically" revealed to the leader.

Gossip

This is not only a fun game but a good lesson in how gossip can change as it spreads.

Ask the guests to sit in a circle. The first (or the leader) whispers something into the ear of the next. (Better make it about a long-gone celebrity so that no germ of slander is even inadvertently dropped that could hurt the victim, even if it's only in fun).

Let's say the "gossip" is: "Did you know that George Washington's teeth were wood, studded with diamonds, that the cherry tree was really an oak, and that Martha Washington once embroidered two tea towels with a secret message that was sent to Valley Forge?"

The next person repeats what he or she thinks was whispered, and so the story goes around the room. If it's like most gossip, it probably will end up something like this, when the last person repeats it aloud:

"Did you know that a spy discovered diamonds hidden in an oak tree at Valley Forge and Martha Washington broke two teeth on a cherry seed when she was embroidering a tea towel for George's inauguration?"

Consequences

This is an old favorite.

Give pencil and paper to each with instructions to write at the top of the page one or two adjectives applying to a woman. The top of the paper is folded down to hide those words and the paper is passed along to the next, who writes a woman's name, folds it, passes it along to the next who writes adjectives describing a man.

The paper goes on around the circle, with each person adding something, until the following crazy-quilt story is complete, with these questions answered:

Adjectives describing a woman
A woman's name
Adjectives describing a man
A man's name
Where they met
What she did
What he did
What she said
What he said
The consequences
What the world said

The hilarious result might read like this:

"The sultry, sirenish Julia Child and the rugged, handsome Abraham Lincoln met at the base of the Sphinx. She put nail polish on a run in her stocking. He did 20 push-ups. She said, 'I have always dreamed of becoming a bareback rider.' He said, 'Dishwashing liquid is so hard on my hands.' They agree to write a fan letter to Fay Wray and the world said, 'Surely, the Franklin automobile will return.'"

Chapter 3
Give More — Get More

Give what you have. To someone, it may be better than you dare to think.

From **Kavanagh**,
by Henry Wadsworth Longfellow

Do as much as you can for somebody else and you'll find you get it back a thousandfold.

Lillian Carter, speaking to the
Pennsylvania Council on Aging

In a midwestern community, senior citizens were told that they could no longer meet in the public school because the space was needed for classes and student activities. But the seniors didn't run out to look for another place. They stayed — and became a part of the school.

Those with special skills became lecturers and teacher's aides. Out of their own work experience and their hobbies came invaluable help for the students, an educational bonus they could not have received from the regular staff. The seniors taught the youngsters about business, about gardening, and about alien lands the pupils had only read about.

Some even joined the school band and took older roles in the school plays.

"This means as much to us as it could ever mean to the students," said one leader. "We are having the time of our life."

So, miles away, was Herman Scott, at 78 one of the happiest and busiest volunteers on the staff of a major hospital. Crippled with arthritis, he used as a walker a grocery cart in which he delivered supplies to various departments.

A former Minnesota school teacher, farmer, plumber, and carpenter, Scott long had dreamed of dropping out of the work force to become a volunteer. He saved enough to support himself for a little while, then took a bus to seek his niche where he would spend the rest of his life. He got off in St. Louis and soon had become a fixture at Cardinal Glennon Memorial Hospital for Children, happily helping patients, writing inspirational poetry and even giving much of his limited income — realized from a few investments — to families or to religious workers in need of financial aid.

Mrs. Lillian Carter, mother of former President Jimmy Carter, traveled much farther than from Minnesota to Missouri to find her place as a volunteer, serving the ill and the hungry in the crowded cities and dusty villages of India. As a Peace Corps worker she found the same joy that Herman Scott discovered in the giant, spotless hospital for children in the middle of America.

"I wanted to treat people who had nothing and do what I could in my declining years," Mrs. Carter said. "It was the greatest experience I ever had."

"There is a tremendous opportunity for retired people in every career and interest field and in many countries of the world," said Ceal Andre, director of the Voluntary Action Center of the United Way of Greater St. Louis.

"Volunteering enriches our lives, adds flavor and excitement to our days. When we are younger, our work is our whole life. When that stops, if we just sit down and do nothing, we are dead.

"The special blessing of volunteer work is that you can do pretty much what you want to do pretty much when and where you want to do it. This doesn't mean that once you have made a commitment you need not keep it. It does mean that you can choose the kind of work you want to do, the neighborhood you want to serve, the hours, the days. Most people don't have that choice in their regular lives.

"And just think of the many ways you can use your skills, enjoy your special interests, or follow your hobby in helping someone else."

The dramatic growth of volunteerism from the Ladies Aid missionary box and Christmas baskets into a more sophisticated national network of skilled and gifted unpaid workers proves that America is not controlled by the dollar sign. From the days of warm, personal philanthropy — and those great-hearted givers were as motivated by love as in the modern volunteer — giving and sharing and serving have been a part of the American way.

But effective volunteerism requires more than a vague love of people and a hunger in the heart to better the quality of life.

Just as in the business world, a qualified person should be matched to a task that he or she is uniquely able to handle, whether by reason of experience, aptitude, physical strength, or available time.

Looking beyond a desire to help others and a willingness to give of yourself, check the following quiz. It is meant to be only a sampling, but it will guide you in choosing a leisure time activity.

— Do you miss your grandchildren and long to have them with you, even though you know that's not possible? Why not be a surrogate grandparent through the Foster Grandparents program or volunteer in a children's home? Could you take over the care of a neighbor's baby for one afternoon a week to let the young mother relax just a bit?

— Do you love the outdoors? Share that love with others. In your city or your neighborhood

are young people, or older ones who don't get around much, who would enjoy going with you on nature hikes or bird walks or just wandering along the river bank or a rustic road picking up unusual rocks or wood or taking snapshots of the outdoors.

— Do you enjoy the search for buried treasure with a metal detector? Take along a small group to help find coins or other objects. If you find a particularly ancient metal piece, say a fragment of farm machinery, conduct a little contest to see who can identify it and figure out its purpose.

— Are you a pretty fair photographer? Set up photography exhibits or small, informal classes in a retirement home or senior center. Organize a snapshot contest but be sure that the standards and awards are fair to beginners as well as to those with a good deal of experience. You may find a former professional photographer living in the home or attending the center. Ask him or her to help you.

Talk with the head of a newspaper photography department and/or the manager of a nearby camera store for guidance, technical advice or, perhaps, to serve as a judge. The newspaper might be willing to print the winning pictures, or the store could give you space for a little public display. The manager, if requested, might be able to work out a reduced price for developing and printing.

— When a catastrophe strikes, do you wish you could help somehow? The Red Cross Disaster Service has a place for you. In the larger cities, retired men stay on duty throughout the night, ready to rush to the scene of a fire or tornado or other disaster to help the affected families.

— Do you love to travel and see the world? A St. Louis couple, while not yet old enough to retire, turned difficulty into opportunity and a chance to see the other side of the globe. The husband's pharmaceutical job was eliminated, and when it appeared that professional opportunities were limited, they accepted an overseas post in India. It meant no money, but expenses were paid, and they were given the opportunity to use their skills to help others — the husband in pharmacy, the wife in the field of family planning.

Through the International Executive Service Corps, retired executives have been sent all over the world to help business and industry — without salary, but with all expenses paid.

— Are you an artist, a would-be artist, a musician, a frustrated actor with the dream of Hollywood or Broadway still lingering in your heart? Your art museum has a place for you as a guide or, perhaps, in the gift shop or bookstore. You would be surrounded every day by the great masters and could hear lectures or take tours when off duty. A nursing home or retirement home needs someone to play the piano, to sing, or to direct a little playlet with residents of the home in the cast.

— Are you a would-be "hoofer" who still remembers the thrill of vaudeville? Get together some of your friends who can sing or dance or play a musical instrument. Then "knock 'em dead and leave 'em laughing" with an old-time vaudeville show. You may not hit the Great White Way, but you'll be stars on the nursing home circuit.

— Are you a writer, an ex-newspaper reporter? Volunteer to turn out publicity releases or start a writing class in a senior center or help residents of a home publish a little newspaper. A big firm in the community may be persuaded to publish the students' writing. The newspaper may be talked into printing the best work.

Such a booklet need not be expensive or elaborate. But it could mean everything in the world to men and women who long to become, at last, "published writers."

Take along a tape recorder, as Jerred Metz did when he visited a senior center and a housing project, seeking to dredge from the residents' memories the compelling and nostalgic stories of their past. From this odyssey emerged a book, "Drinking the Dipper Dry."

"Here were people," said Metz, "with a desire to share, not to convince or persuade. They laughed at each other's stories. They were saddened."

You, like the poet Metz, can help older people preserve the tales of yesterday as a precious legacy for their children and grandchildren.

So what have you to offer? A special skill? Time? Experience? Are you outgoing or a private person? Agencies need quiet, meticulous office workers as well as enthusiastic, uninhibited mixers.

If you can't face certain tasks, don't be embarrassed. Not everyone can stand the sight of blood or illness. It's nothing to be ashamed of.

But there is a job to fit your skills and your interests and your abilities.

You are needed. You are a special person.

"To someone, it may be better than you dare to think."

Chapter 4
Write On!

Have you often longed to write? Have you a story you are eager to tell? Now that you have the time, do you hesitate because you think you haven't the talent? Just remember that every successful writer began with just one word. So can you.

Seated around a table in a little room of the public library, they were laughing so hard that the teacher of a class next door had to ask them to be quiet. The laughter was muffled a bit, throttled down to smiles and giggles, but the joy didn't disappear.

This was a class in writing for older adults, and they were having the time of their life.

Every Saturday morning they gathered — some 15 of them — to talk about writing, to share their work and, with wry smiles, to read their rejection letters. Their inability to sell hadn't dampened their enthusiasm or their hope that someday they would be published authors.

But even if their stories or poems or articles would never be printed in a magazine or newspaper, so what? For the time being, although serious in their quest, they were simply enjoying a creative session and a rare camaraderie over coffee and doughnuts. They had met as strangers with a common dream of learning to write or to polish the skills they already owned. But now they were good friends.

Most had never written before, and they were timid about trying. But within a few weeks, those who had only wanted to "observe" were joining the give-and-take, bringing in their own work, accepting with grace the gentle criticism and supportive praise.

They came from everywhere, and each enriched the group. One was a retired physician. Two had owned beauty salons. One was a retired postal worker, one a retired school teacher. One had moved to the United States from Hungary. Their class, sponsored by the Arts for Older Adults program of an educational laboratory, was taught by a professional newspaper feature writer.

This class was in St. Louis. But similar groups are forming throughout America.

They're waiting for you.

How do you start?

1. Check your newspaper, your telephone directory, your church, the board of education, the Adult Education Council, or any community agency on aging for information on daytime or evening classes. The fee usually is nominal.

2. If you're timid about joining a group of strangers (but remember that they'll soon be your friends), ask two or three or four of your close acquaintances to get together on a regular basis to write or talk about writing. One such group in the midwest meets informally one Sunday afternoon a month. Within a year of its organization, one member had sold three articles and another had sold two. They credit the support of and stimulation by others in the group for their successful efforts.

3. Such an informal group can be organized in a retirement home or among shut-ins. (See Chapter 9.) Check with agencies on aging or with newspapers in your city for suggested names of volunteer teachers.

4. If you can't find anyone to share your hobby, go it alone. It won't be as much fun, because writing, as millions have discovered, is

a lonely business. But just to put on paper some words that will cheer or bless or help someone — an idea or message that will touch another human being — will bring you untold joy.

So, whether you are working alone or with others, how do you start to write a story?

Begin with an idea. Be sure that you know what you want to say. Words without an idea are like icing without a cake or butter without bread.

Write your idea, as contest entrants do, in "25 words or less." This will help you focus on a narrow, manageable topic. Let's say, for example, that you want to write about antiques. That's a tremendous subject, so you must cull from it a specific segment. "How to Begin a Collection of Antique Clocks" might be the title of an article. Another might be, "What to Look for at an Antiques Auction."

The important thing is to zero in on a concrete, narrow idea.

But where do you get that idea? From everywhere. From your memories. From your own kitchen. From a conversation with a neighbor. From a problem that calls for a solution. The list goes on and on.

Many retirees want to write nostalgic pieces. That's fine. Historical magazines are looking for good stories about the past.

But don't limit yourself to recreating yesterday. The market for stories of today is much better.

So ask yourself: "What am I qualified to write about? Children? Food? Mechanical engineering? Fashion? Antiques? Music?"

Even tragedy can lead to a writing avocation.

Betty Pavlige, an early semiretiree, found her writing career in heartache. Betty works part time in her beauty salon, which she has turned over to her daughter in order to have more time for her hobbies of writing and painting.

Distressed by the death of a family member, a victim of alcoholism, she prepared a helpful paper for use in counseling families of alcoholics.

"I know that I was inspired," she said. "It could not have happened any other way, because I knew absolutely nothing about writing. I just felt that there was something inside of me that had to come out."

Some months later, as she was setting a customer's hair, she suddenly felt that compulsion anew — as though divinely led — to write something about her childhood and the historic area in which she and her family had lived.

"I couldn't help myself," she said. "I walked to the other side of the salon, picked up a paper and pad, and started writing."

In a few minutes Betty returned to her customer but, thereafter, in every free moment, she would go back to that corner of the salon and write more.

The result is **Growing Up in Soulard,** a delightful and warm memoir of her days in South St. Louis, published in 1980 (211 pages) by Knight Publishing Co., 3552 Crittenden, St. Louis, Mo. 63118.

Betty is still writing, but not about the past. Her next story was about the lonely characters she had seen at a park.

Avis Dungan Carlson, of St. Louis, also reached back into her childhood for writing inspiration. She literally took a packet of memories from a trunk in the attic and transformed it into a book, **Small World, Long Gone** (The Schorf Press, Evanston, Ill. $6.95). Another of her books, "In the Fullness of Time" (Henry Regnery Co., Chicago), recalled the unhappy dust bowl-depression days of the early 1930s.

But Mrs. Carlson did not wait until her family was grown to begin writing. She sold her first article to Harper's Magazine when she was in her 20s, and 60 years later was still at her typewriter, sandwiching her writing between her teaching and community responsibilities. In her 80s, she began a new chapter of her career as a columnist for a major metropolitan newspaper.

However, her books might not have been published had it not been for the persistence and encouragement of her son.

Listening to her childhood stories, he told her, "That life you lived is gone. It won't come again. So put it down for my sister and me."

"That winter," she said, "when my husband and I went to Florida, I put a typewriter, a dictionary, and a thesaurus in the car. When we returned three months later, much of **Small World, Long Gone** was finished."

It was meant only for the eyes of her children and was stored away in a trunk, "waiting for me to die."

But the manuscript didn't stay there, thanks to one of those seeming coincidences every successful writer has experienced.

She had written what she thought would be a series of magazine articles reflecting her anger at the treatment of older people during the depression years and the tragic effects of the dust bowl on the lives of midwesterners. An agent, whom she met while on a visit to her son's home, suggested that instead of a series they be published as a book. This became **In the Fullness of Time.**

The agent then asked to see her other writing, and **Small World, Long Gone** came out of the trunk. It is the warm and bittersweet story of hardship and joy, humor and love in her family life in the Flint Hills of Kansas.

Retirees should write of such things, Mrs. Carlson said. They should record the histories of their families.

"Our time will be gone and gone forever unless we record some of these stories," she continued. "We have a legacy to leave."

The late Ruth Philpott Collins also wrote with tenderness and humor of her cherished family. But, in addition, she wrote serials and homemaking hints, children's stories, advice columns, detective yarns, and religious articles, which she sold to various kinds of publications, scholarly and popular. (See Ruth P. Collins, **The Mystery of the Giant Giraffe,** Henry Z. Walck, Inc., Div. of David McKay Co. Inc., Promotion Dept., 750 Third Ave., N.Y., N.Y. 10017.)

Ruth, outgoing, observant, and blessed with the spirit of joyous adventure and with a deep, abiding faith, the gift of laughter and all-encompassing love, was still turning out yarns and articles until shortly before her death at 84.

She always kept a pencil and pad in her pocket or purse and by her bed in order to jot down every idea. She found those ideas every-where — on her own street, in the teeming cities of India, in her kitchen, her church — even on her bus journeys through Arkansas to visit members of her family. She marketed hundreds of articles and short stories as well as a number of books, drawing on her life experiences and her observations to turn her gift into gold.

You, too, can find that gold if you make sure to submit to a newspaper or magazine what the editor and the readers want. Visit the reading room of your public library. Study the magazines that interest you and that you think you might like to write for. See what subjects are covered. Check the length of the articles. Study the style as well as content.

Obtain either at the library or at a bookstore a reference work such as **Writer's Market** (Published by Writer's Digest Books, 9983 Alliance Rd., Cincinnati, Ohio 45242). Here you will find the names of thousands of publications and their special needs and requirements. Then be sure to follow the editorial suggestions and instructions as to length, style, and content.

But don't let your natural and understandable desire to see your name in print rob you of the simple joy of building a story, poem, feature, or prayer with words chosen carefully, just as an artisan chooses his stones as he builds a cathedral.

Discover the delicate nuances of meaning. Dig new, colorful, vigorous words out of the dictionary. Savor them. Make their beauty and muscle your own. You will find much inspiration in the writings of Shakespeare and Dickens and in the Bible.

Then, as you build your sentences word by word and thought by thought, hold them in your mind as you would hold a lump of clay in your hands, turning it, patting it, caressing it, shaping it into something lovely, lean, and strong to be remembered, relished, and enjoyed by another.

Whether your words shout or whisper, inspire or comfort, remember that they may touch some life.

This can be your adventure. Look for the right idea as a treasure hunter searches for buried gold in the South Seas. It will take patience and persistence, but, once having found it, write on!

Chapter 5
The Happy Wanderers

Elva Norman, 67, trekked for miles up and down treacherous trails in the mountains of Nepal. She was separated for a time from her son — the only person she knew in that part of the world — by a monsoon that turned the skies to indigo and the roads to dark brown slush. She slept in primitive huts, climbed into a forbidden palace courtyard to use the village's only telephone and later landed in the middle of a revolution.

On that strange adventure she shared the trails with hundreds of lowly, gentle Nepalese, made friendships that will last a lifetime, and met Sir Edmund Hillary, the doughty New Zealander who in 1953 climbed into the frozen silences of the Himalayas to become the first to scale Mt. Everest's 29,028 forbidding feet.

She returned with vivid, happy memories that will never fade out of her mind and heart, and, as a journalist, with abundant material for free-lance articles and for a book.

Mrs. Norman, a St. Louis widow and mother of three, might have been persuaded to stay in the safety and comfort of her own home by the warning of her youngest son, Tom, a one-time Peace Corps teacher in Nepal, that the "cultural shock" could be too much for her to take.

She refused to be afraid.

For this vivacious senior citizen, it was not an easy trip. She lived for weeks in a primitive, unsophisticated society. She ate strange foods. She encountered unfamiliar customs. But it was rewarding beyond measure.

"My life was wonderfully enriched by that trip," she said. "Adventure is not just for the young. I did meet some young people there, and that added to the flavor of the whole experience. But I also met men and women my age, people from many countries who were trekking or who had pulled up roots and established a new way of life in that strange land.

"There were times when only faith brought me through. I can remember how frightened I was when I had to cross a raging river on a 50-foot-long log that was only one foot wide. I prayed to be taken safely across, and I made it. I knew, in that moment, that God was watching over me.

"We all need to pack our faith in God along with our clothes and our cosmetics.

"Travel to some unfamiliar, exotic land isn't for everyone. Not even all young people would enjoy it. But for those of any age who aren't afraid to venture off the beaten path, it can be a wonderfully joyous and exciting experience."

Maybe you haven't the time or the money or the physical stamina — or think you haven't — to travel across the world. But don't reject it out of hand.

Get the atlas down from the shelf. Dust it off. Study it. Now take your dreams out of cold storage.

Where have you often longed to go?

London? Paris? Nova Scotia? Nepal? China? Russia? Africa?

Have you been dreaming of an ancestral treasure hunt? Would you like to dig for family roots in France, Germany, Yugoslavia, or Italy?

All right. Now — right this moment — think about it. Is there a valid reason why you can't at least consider it?

Money?

Certainly, it costs money. Doesn't everything these days? It may cost even more next year. Make up a travel budget. If you haven't enough right now, start saving. Do you **NEED** that new coat or fishing rod or stereo? Put the money instead into a special "going away" account. As much as you love your children or grandchildren, do they **NEED** the money you may be saving for them? There's nothing wrong about spending for yourself instead of making unnecessary (perhaps unappreciated?) sacrifices.

Check into the many senior citizen discounts offered by organizations, travel agencies, clubs, churches, fraternal groups, alumni associations. Talk to the airlines. Think about a freighter trip that could take you on a slow boat to those faraway places with strange sounding names.

You may find that it costs less than you feared.

All right. What else is holding you back?

Your health?

If you are in reasonably good health, ask your doctor. Perhaps he or she will approve either unlimited travel or give you the go-ahead with certain restrictions.

Time?

If you are still employed, have you some accrued vacation? Can't you find a substitute to fill in at church or club or the weekly bridge session?

No one to go with you?

How do you know if you don't ask? A good friend, a nephew, a grandchild, a neighbor, a business associate may just be hoping and dreaming of such a trip.

Whether you go alone or with a travel partner, you probably would be wise to consider a tour rather than striking out on your own (unless, of course, you are a seasoned and self-sufficient traveler). The tour guide takes care of luggage, keeps the group together, handles emergencies.

For the sake of companionship or economy, single travelers can be assigned rooms together. Before you say a quick yes or no to such an arrangement, think it over from all standpoints.

You two may hit it off perfectly and forge a friendship that will last long after the trip is over. But even if you find that you thoroughly enjoy one another's company, don't become a twosome and exclude others. Neither should feel compelled to change plans or schedules or waking-up or going-to-bed habits just to please the other. Even with a good buddy, independence is too precious to throw away for the sake of harmony.

If you discover, after the trip begins, that you can't stand each other, ask the tour guide to make other arrangements, even if you have to pay a little extra. Don't let disharmony mar your trip.

Most of us, of course, have learned that life is full of compromises. If we don't see eye to eye with another, we can make allowances. With a bit of understanding — and, perhaps, with a great deal of prayer for patience and compassion — we can live with minor irritations. Remember, too, that the other person is "putting up" with you. Harmony is a two-way street.

So now that you have considered money and time and companionship, what is keeping you from the trip of your dreams?

Fear?

What are you afraid of?

Illness? Accident? As long as you are not traveling alone in the desert wastes or standing in solitary glory atop a snow-covered mountain, why should you be any more afraid of an emergency abroad than you would be at home?

Running out of money? Not if you budget wisely and refuse to spend on gimcracks you don't want or need.

Not having a good time? If you don't, it probably will be your own fault. The whole, wide, wonderful world is out there for you to see and enjoy. If you pack an expectant attitude with your clothes, your cosmetics — and your faith — nothing can rob you of your joy.

But let's look at a dream through real-colored glasses. Maybe you do not have the money or the stamina to take an overseas tour.

What are the alternatives?

Before you even begin to think about those, make this promise to yourself:

"Even though I may no longer have the energy I had as a teenager, even though I must watch my pennies, I will not lock myself behind my front door and cheat myself out of excitement, adventure, and fun.

"While I have life, I will live it. So help me God!"

Now for those alternatives.

How about a bus trip? Investigate special rates. Call the organizations for senior citizens in your community. They often plan special tours. Cross-country busses are quite comfortable, as a rule. They are air-conditioned and equipped with running water and toilet facilities and with comfortable seats that can be pushed back, so that you can stretch your feet and snooze. But with the world passing by your window, you won't want to close your eyes too often or too long.

How about a train trip? Remember how much you enjoyed the trains as a child or teenager? They may not be as sleek or as fast or as luxurious as formerly, but the thrill of speeding across the countryside from coach or parlor car seat can be yours for little money.

Perhaps, you really can't get out of town.

All right. How about a trip **in** town?

Haven't you often wanted to investigate the farmer's market or the antique shops on the other side of the city? What about your old neighborhood? Ask a good friend to take an adventure with you — and hop aboard.

Even with the high price of gasoline and motels, an automobile trip can be fun. You can stick to the highway or you can wander off on little country roads to small towns tucked away and almost forgotten. Take your camera. You may find a historic monument or grave marker or bridge about which you could write a good story for a newspaper or magazine.

Don't be afraid to strike out. But do use wisdom. You will enjoy it more with a group, and it's probably wise to have at least one man in the party. (If a woman motorist has a flat tire, she shouldn't expect the man to do **all** the work of changing it, but he usually knows more about mechanical things than she does.)

If you take such a trip by car, have a destination and a schedule — not too tight! — so you will really accomplish something and see what you want to see. Look for the unusual. Find good places to eat. Keep the conversation happy and uplifting. Make a rule before starting out that no one is to discuss aches and pains.

Have you relatives or good friends in a near-by town? Whether or not you plan to stay over-night with them, ask them to have a meal with you and your party and show you some of the unusual sights in that area.

But no matter whether you travel by air or train or car or cross-country or cross-city bus, take to the road. Pack away your fears and follow your dream.

Adventure was never meant to be an easy path without a few stones to stumble over. But all the world is waiting out there to be discovered and savored and loved.

What if we don't have all the money or time or companionship we need and want? Let's make the most of what we have.

Dr. Paul S. McElroy, an ardent senior citizen explorer of the world around him, wrote in the **St. Louis Globe-Democrat:**

"Adversity may force us to be more efficient, more economical — and when our reserves are limited our ingenuity may be sharpened — for necessity is the mother of invention, and this may prove a blessing. The problems which the changes (in the 1980s) may bring may become challenges which, in turn, may be the very means of enabling us to develop our resources and strengthen our character. . . .

"There is reason for hope as the demands of the '80s force us to become aware, in ways we have not experienced before, of our dependence upon the Giver of Every Good and Perfect Gift, the Ruler of the Universe."

Dr. McElroy, who as a younger man climbed 19,340-foot Mt. Kilimanjaro in Tanzania, almost on impulse, traveled to China long after he had retired as a Congregational minister. Even though he no longer preaches every Sunday, he writes minisermons as a columnist for a daily newspaper.

His advice to all others of his generation is summed up in the title of his column and of his book:

Live a Little More 1978, Peter Pauper Press, 135 W. 50th Street, N.Y., N.Y. 10028.

Chapter **6**

Happy Hobby Days

No man is really happy or safe without a hobby, and it makes precious little difference what the outside interest may be....anything will do so long as he straddles a hobby and rides it hard.

Sir William Osler, Aphorisms From
His Bedside Teachings and Writings
in **The Crown Treasury of Relevant
Quotations,** ©Copyright 1978
Edward F. Murray (New York:
Crown Publishers Inc., 1978)
New York 10019

What would you like to do?

Talk to someone across the world? Discover a buried treasure? Find a rare stamp? Build an old-time crystal radio? Take apart an old clock and put it back in running order? Write a radio show — or star in it? Join a band or a symphony orchestra?

You can.

Would you like to collect autographs of country music stars or old comic books or postcards or barbed wire? Do you want to know more about Abraham Lincoln, Theodore Roosevelt, or the battles of the Civil War?

What's stopping you?

Do you enjoy working with your hands? Would you like to make lovely furniture? Do you want to create delicate, porcelain eggs or make a quilt for your grandchild? Have you ever wanted to be a clown in a circus, sing in a glee club, or build a model car?

Why not?

You have the time now, the time you were longing for all those years of alarm clocks, schedules, bosses, and three-week vacations. So use it. Don't throw away what could be the prime of your life. Don't sit down now and forget how to stand up. As retired St. Louis merchant J. Arthur Baer II says, "It's foolish to turn off the faucet just because you hit a certain age" (The **St. Louis Globe-Democrat,** July 25-26, 1981, page 1B).

If you think of your 65th birthday only as a magic milestone that separates the slavery of work and the freedom of leisure, watch out. You may just trip over that milestone and land right out in the middle of the pasture watching the rest of the world go by.

OK— you don't have a lot of money and not too much muscle. So? You're not alone. But your mind isn't thin because your purse is, and your heart hasn't slowed down because your body has.

Now if the problem is money, you have three choices: You can (1) turn your hobby into gold, (2) choose one that requires little investment, or (3) decide it's not worth the candle and go on out to that pasture.

Many a retiree has started a leisure time interest for fun and has found a fortune. Others have upped retirement incomes with part-time jobs. Those stories are told in Chapter 7.

But whether you want a hobby for profit or just for pleasure, you'll find many that cost little. For a small fee, or, perhaps, none at all, you can go back to school to study any subject you wish, from astronomy to zoology. The public library, that bottomless treasure chest of information, is free. It doesn't cost you a cent to study the stars. The beauty of nature is God's gift to man.

A hobby need not require physical strength, energy, or the ability to travel. But whether it is for the active or the quiet, for the home-based or the retiree-on-the-go, a hobby is an antidote for the poison of boredom. Get involved, and you'll feel better. You'll find more excitement and joy than you thought existed in this muddled and sometimes miserable world.

In his research for **The World Almanac Book of Buffs, Masters, Mavens and Uncommon Experts** (Copyright 1980 by Newspaper Enterprise Association N.Y., N.Y.) Henry Doering developed a hobby of his own — discovering unique hobbyists. He ferreted out an amazing variety of interests, ranging from Great Lakes steamboats to juggling and from the Aaron Burr Association to World War II military currency.

"It seems like the more leisure time we have," he wrote, "the less we do with it. We thought that if we could talk to a group of individuals who live life to its fullest, and find out what spurred them into action, that it might prove contagious.

"We don't think we're alone. We believe that thousands of Americans would gladly use their free time more constructively if they could be exposed to the pleasures that other folks enjoy, and had specific facts on how they, too, can blossom into buffs, mavens and experts."

Doering interviewed thousands of hobbyists. He found an amazing range of interests. The world of hobbies is like a supermarket full of wonderful products, some far more expensive than others.

At your public library you will find whole sections of books on almost any hobby you can think of, and the magazine room will provide up-to-date information and guidance on everything from accordions and aerospace to zeppelins and zinnias. America is a multi-fragmented society and tiny and large groups are drawn together by their common interests.

Here are three that have attracted thousands of aficionadoes: ham radio, building model cars or collecting car advertising brochures, and looking for buried treasure.

The first requires money — though it can be a modest investment — and some basic technical skills. The second is for the the home-based as well as the more active, and you can spend as much or as little as you wish. For the third, you will need the strength to operate a metal detector, which you can buy for as little as $25 or $30 or as much as several hundred dollars. Obviously, the more sophisticated the detector, the better your chances of finding valuables, but you could get back your investment on one treasure-hunting expedition.

With ham radio as your hobby, you won't find coins, but you'll find friends all over the world. In the 1972 (Volume XV, p. 13) issue of **Rehabilitation Gazette** (sub-titled: The International Journal for Independent Living by Disabled People), Ernest Kirschten wrote:

"How can a man be lonely while talking to an anthropologist in New Guinea, an archaeologist in Tanzania, a botanist in the Galapagos, a marine biologist on Easter Island, a missionary in the Congo, a factory worker in Yugoslavia, a university professor in India, a housewife in Japan, a ski instructor in Switzerland, a nuclear physicist on Amchitka, a technical school student in Moscow, a priest in the Vatican, a South American lady who lives on top of her own diamond mine, a Russian explorer in Antarctica with the temperature 142 degrees below zero, an American doctor at a missionary hospital in the Niger Republic with the temperature 142 degrees above zero, a NASA radar technician at a tracking station in Madagascar, the Honorable Barry Goldwater of Arizona and a King, His Majesty Hussein the First of Jordan?

"This reflects only part of the log of Lex Frieden."

Frieden, now of Houston, Tex., is a quadriplegic, the paralyzed victim of an automobile accident. A staunch advocate of independent living, he travels extensively despite his physical condition, but he would be the first to say that for anyone, active or home-based, ham radio can open a window on the world.

You can get started on this hobby with a used, low-powered code transmitter at a cost of a few hundred dollars. What you spend later would depend on the technical sophistication you desire.

But before you can go on the air, you must be licensed by the Federal Communications Commission. Check your Federal building to learn where to write for information.

Ham radio operators have saved lives, solved crimes, and sent emergency messages all over the world. In every major disaster, they set up the first communications network.

J. Russell Dye, a retired St. Louis newspaperman, received and relayed numerous calls about victims in the tragic earthquake in Guatemala. But his transmitter and receiver also keep him in touch with old friends, all of whom are retired and many of whom live in faraway parts of the country.

"Every weekday morning at 10, we all get on the air and talk for an hour or so," Dye said. "We knew each other as ham operators back in the 1930s and 1940s, and, now that we are scattered, we have formed this round table to keep in touch with each other over the air."

One of those morning conversations led Dye into a second hobby — working with stained glass and creating Tiffany-like lamps. He has become so proficient that he sells his work and occasionally teaches classes to other retirees.

"A man in our round table does this and he started talking about it and I just got interested.

"You have to have a certain artistic sense to know what colors and types of glass fit together and how to create a design," Dye said. "But you can get into the hobby without spending a lot of money. You will need a soldering iron and then, of course, you buy the sheets of glass."

Dye learned the skill, beginning with simple suncatchers and progressing to lamps, at an adult evening class and later attended specialized art courses.

Another newspaperman, Don Hammonds, Urban Affairs reporter for the **St. Louis Globe-Democrat,** is many years from retirement, but he already is preparing for it by following a number of hobbies.

"I am not willing to sit down and do nothing," he said. "I believe the later years, if you have some special interests you have developed, can be the greatest of your life.

"My main hobby is cars," said the 30-year-old bachelor. "I started that literally when I was 2, and I expect to keep on with it until I'm 102.

"My parents tell me my first word was 'Ford,' and that long before I was ready for kindergarten I was fascinated by pictures of automobiles."

Today, Hammonds has a collection of nearly 2,000 sales room catalogs. For the past 15 or 20 years he has obtained them himself, at no cost, by simply walking into a showroom and asking for them. The older ones he has bought or traded for.

"You can buy them for maybe $15," he said, "but some are now worth 10 times that amount."

A related hobby is making model cars.

"That doesn't cost much," Hammonds pointed out. "You will need a knife and glue and kits that sell for a few dollars.

"You can find kits for all kinds of cars. An older person could recreate a miniature of his or her first family car, a Model-T, a Packard or a Studebaker.

"You can buy scale models or toy cars or you can make them from scratch, designing your own."

A collector or designer, Hammonds said, can even build a track and have road races or drag races. Information on all facets of this hobby is available from the public library or in magazines on the news stands.

No hobby has ·sparked more legend and lore, more hope and heartbreak, than the search for buried treasure. For some, it's a weekend adventure or a Saturday outing. For others, it's big business.

Treasure hunting can take you just as far as your own backyard, to see if you can find some stray coins or, perhaps, a ring lost by a former tenant. Or it can take you to the floor of the Atlantic Ocean, where you can spend millions of dollars, literally, to bring long-lost ships laden with gold to the surface. Its rewards can range from a worthless bottle cap to a sunken Spanish galleon.

To get started on a modest scale, check out metal detectors at a sporting goods or electronics store. Then go hunting and remember, as a St. Louis reporter wrote, that "just beneath the next growl of the metal detector, buried deep in the earth and long forgotten, may be a Revolutionary War belt buckle, a silver teapot from the Santa Maria or, at least, an 1876 Indian Head penny in perfect condition.

"Never mind that the belt buckle may turn out to be a rusty spark plug, the silver teapot a soft drink can, or the Indian Head penny a 1969 Roosevelt dime.

"There's always another plot to be surveyed, another hole to be dug, a strike to be made, an instant fortune to be plucked out of its earthy prison."

You may find a dozen valuable coins on a single trip or you may find nothing. You may run across a Spanish coin worth thousands, or you may end your search with four rusty nails and a bent penny.

Never mind. You'll find fun and adventure. And isn't that what a hobby is all about?

But having found a treasure, be it large or small, or built a collection, be it elaborate or modest, you can share the joy of the search with others.

Through your own — or another's — artistic and writing talents, you can create an exciting and educational slide show, even with narration, music, or sound effects on a tape to be synchronized with the slides.

Such a show, or a simpler, standing exhibit can be a wonderfully welcome program for an adult or youth group at your church. It can mean even more to them if you can give at least a part of your hobby a religious significance.

A stamp enthusiast might have one collection of Madonnas to illustrate how various artists have depicted the Mother and Child. Read up on the artists themselves. What convictions or influences inspired their interest in religious art?

Another religious collection might be stamps of countries related to Biblical history.

If you collect coins, even though you can't

afford ancient pieces, try to find pictures or sketches of historic money, and build a slide show or exhibit. Your church group would enjoy learning about the coins of Biblical times and why religious mottoes or inscriptions — such as "In God we trust" — appear on certain moneys.

Enhance your hobby by sharing it with others. The adventure and the joy will be multiplied many times over.

Chapter 7
There's Gold in the Golden Years

To the nostalgic strains of big band music, Charlie Menees (former reporter for the **St. Louis Post-Dispatch,** also former editor for the McDonnell Douglas Corp. newspaper) turned his hobby into retirement gold by becoming a disc jockey.

Carl Otto, a successful lawyer and former assistant attorney general of the State of Missouri, decided to return to the family manufacturing business in which he had grown up and before long had risen to the top of his industry. Some years later, in his 70s and semi-retired, he revitalized another company in the same manufacturing field, moved it to a new site, and went back on the road, selling its products across the world.

When she was 87, Ruth Hutchinson resumed a radio career she had begun after retirement from a clerical post, and was billed as "the country's oldest disc jockey."

At 82, Eva Le Gallienne was still active in the theater, nominated for an Oscar for her role in the movie, **Resurrection.**

At 85, R. Buckminster Fuller, philosopher, inventor, and innovative architect, was still an outspoken advocate of the geodesic dome as an energy saver and was continuing to envision and strike out for new horizons.

The Rev. Dr. Paul S. McElroy, retired Congregational minister, kept up an active writing career after leaving the pulpit. With more than 20 books to his credit, he launched a semiweekly inspirational column in a metropolitan newspaper, the **St. Louis Globe-Democrat,** and his writings were compiled in a book, **Live a Little More,** its title a reflection of his philosophy and his enthusiasm for life.

The Rev. Betty R. Bailey, a Presbyterian minister who retired early because of throat surgery, happened into a shell hobby shop one day. The visit transformed her into an ardent shell collector, and soon she was selling many of the artistic pieces she created in her home.

Francis Frederick retired after 30 years from the postal service at 65 but kept right on working in the same field. He is assigned to duty every other week in a university mail room.

William Zalken, a former general manager of the St. Louis Municipal Opera and the St. Louis Symphony Orchestra, maintains an office for his retirement career of public relations consultant.

They are among the millions of older Americans who have panned for gold in their later years and have struck it rich — if not always in money, at least in satisfaction. They are the new breed of retiree who doesn't want to stop working.

According to the **Wall Street Journal** (July 22, 1981), the experience of a major insurance company "suggests that old Americans have strikingly changed their attitudes toward retirement."

Thirty years ago, the paper reported, a survey found that 90 percent of older people wanted to retire early, but a recent study by the company showed that only 12 percent of the employees wanted to retire before 62, and 22 percent wanted to work after 65.

With the pressures of inflation, money is one big reason why thousands of retirees on fixed pensions or dependent on social security are looking for part-time jobs. But that is not the only reason. Gold comes in many forms — fun, involvement, satisfaction, the joy of helping someone, the exhilaration of proving self-worth.

"Fishing is not my thing," said the exuberant "Willie" Zalken. "I enjoy keeping my fingers in the pie" **(St. Louis Globe-Democrat,** July 25-26, 1981, page 1B).

He has advice to others who hit the magic marker of 65.

"Keep your minds open and your feet active. Don't sit and mope. Retirement is inevitable for everyone. Enjoy it to the fullest."

His words were echoed by another retiree, Dan J. Forrestal, former president of the Public Relations Society of America. An ex-newspaperman and public relations director of Monsanto Co., Forrestal is writing books and consulting with major companies on public relations activities.

"If retirement means fishing or sitting in a rocking chair, then I'm definitely not retired," he said in an interview with the **St. Louis Globe-Democrat** (July 25-26, 1981, page 1B). "I equate enjoyability with involvement, activity and staying in the mainstream of life."

Dr. McElroy finds retirement the same kind of challenge he faced years ago when he decided, almost on the spur of the moment, to climb awesome Mount Kilimanjaro.

"But we all need a challenge," he said. "If we just sit around in retirement and do nothing, we become depressed."

He wrote in his book, **Live a Little More** (page 57):

"We must not look for approval and appreciation from others as a sign that we are on the right path. We must adhere to our own convictions as though we were alone in the world and not be guided by the wishes of others but remain inner-directed."

But for many, the bottom line is money. So if you need to supplement your retirement income, here are some suggestions from employment counselors:

1. Talk to your former employer about a part-time job. It's possible you would have an inside track because you and your work are known.

2. Apply at the Employment Service and private agencies and check out the classified ads.

3. Turn your special skills or your hobby into a money-maker.

4. Buy into an established company or start a new one, preferably in your own field. If you have never worked in a food establishment, for example, don't rush out to buy or start a restaurant. You may run into tremendous financial and operational headaches.

5. Don't be reluctant to let your friends know that you want to work, even that you **need** a job. Put out feelers — at your former company, at social agencies, at your church, your club, your neighborhood school. Drop in to see the building manager in the next block or the head of the supermarket or the shoe shop, the doctor, dentist, and lawyer.

6. If you have held an executive job, specialized agencies help locate managerial posts.

But before you go job-hunting, at whatever level, how do you prepare yourself?

By remembering the four A's — appearance, approach, appraisal, attitude.

An applicant should not have to be reminded to wear a good business suit or a quiet-patterned jacket and slacks, with a clean shirt and a tie that's not too loud. A woman should wear a dark, simple dress or suit. Pant suits may be appropriate for the job, but it is better to wear a skirt when applying for it.

But approach and attitude are as important as appearance.

Approach a job interview with your head high and your shoulders back. No matter how low or discouraged you feel, don't let the potential employer know it. Try to imagine yourself on the other side of the desk. You would want an applicant to reflect a blend of self-confidence, poise, and candor, to be absolutely honest, willing to consider whatever work was available, neither downgrading his or her abilities nor exaggerating them.

Before you go into an interview, take a deep breath, stand up with pride, and say to yourself: "I am a child of God. Therefore I am a person of worth. I may not have the skills needed for this particular job, but somewhere, an employer needs what I can contribute. Regardless of the outcome here, I will be pleasant and courteous, and I will not be discouraged."

But before asking for the job, you should already have taken two important steps: (1) analyze, with honesty, your own strengths and weaknesses, and (2) appraise the company to which you are applying. Is it stable or fly-by-night? Would you be proud to say you worked there? Are its products and services in keeping with your own personal tastes, convictions, and ethical standards?

Once there, be what you are — no more, no less. Don't pass yourself off as an accountant if you can hardly balance a checkbook. On the other hand, never walk into a job interview with a hangdog look and announce silently, if not audibly, that you have no talent and no faith in your ability and that you are not worth hiring.

Remember that you have much to offer:

skill, experience, maturity, and integrity.

Never sell yourself and your unique qualities short.

Don't sell a job short either.

Don't ever think — let alone say aloud — that you are "just" something or other. Every job can be endowed with dignity and responsibility. If you think, for example, that you may be qualified as a receptionist, remember that the receptionist is the "front" for the company, and even though he or she may not have technical skills, it is an important post worthy of one's best efforts (as is every job). If you're going to downgrade a job as unimportant for someone of your experience, don't take it. You'll never succeed at it.

Many retirees are messengers or delivery persons. Men, especially, enjoy this work because it gets them outdoors, gives them physical activity and yet is not too demanding. But these are essential jobs, and if you take one, even though you are qualified for more responsible office tasks, don't be hurt or offended if you encounter discourtesy. Rudeness is the culprit's problem, not the so-called "victim's."

So, what **are** you qualified for? What jobs fit in with your experience, your talents, your leisure-time interests, your physical condition?

Sometimes, it seems as though you just fall into a job. Ruth Hutchinson, who had retired from a clerical position, was visiting the radio station where her daughter was employed and, at the daughter's suggestion, auditioned for a commercial requiring an "elderly" voice. She did so well that she was given her own radio show. Illness forced her off the air for several years, but at 87 she was back, garnering a whole new crop of fans.

Hers is a happy and a rare success story. Such fun jobs are not plentiful, so you may have to start at a less glamorous level, even though you have certain gifts that would fit you for an entertainment career.

Make use of every talent and skill you have. You never know when it might turn into gold.

Charlie Menees' interest in music began when he was a youngster in Illinois, where he played trombone, drums, and piano and had his own band. Even though he became a highly successful journalist, music remained his avocation. He was St. Louis' first disc jockey specializing in big band music and appeared for many years on local stations even while holding down a full-time job on a newspaper and later in public relations.

"But it was all given away," he said, "because I loved it so much. Now that I am retired, I am being paid for it for the first time. And, with inflation, that's important."

Don't be afraid to dream a bit, just as Menees did as a boy. But temper your dreams with realism.

Are you an accomplished musician? Have you built, as Menees did, a large collection of records? If you cannot be a radio star, you could play the piano or play your records for church functions, as a volunteer, or in a restaurant, for pay.

Betty Bailey did not expect to make a fortune selling lovely shell-decorated boxes and clocks and frames and other pieces. But it did add to her retirement income even though, to her, the greatest rewards were the feeling of being useful, the awareness of self-worth in the creation of beautiful articles, and the total involvement of one's mind and hands. "You get so wrapped up in something like this," she said, "that you don't know what time it is."

Francis Frederick knew he wouldn't earn as much as when he was working full time in the postal service, but he accepted the part-time job because "it keeps me mentally alert and physically in condition."

Many other retirees have fashioned whole new careers out of their hobbies or past professional experience.

A Texas woman began collecting old furniture many years ago. Now she makes slipcovers and draperies, puts new cane, rush, and splint seats on old chairs, and upholsters and refinishes battered pieces from the past in a thriving late-life enterprise.

An Illinois lawyer whose hobby was photography got in touch with all the schools and churches in his community and now has created a sizable retirement business. He takes all the class pictures and has persuaded several churches to publish a roster of their members, with individual photographs. Many members have ordered extra prints for themselves.

A professional photographer who no longer wanted to maintain a busy shop requiring his attention every day, developed a specialty of photographing pets. His work is in demand not only in his home city but throughout the area. He can make appointments pretty much at his own convenience and take days off or vacations when he wishes. If he drives more than 40 miles from his home, he charges mileage in addition to his regular fee. He also watches for announcements of pet shows and gets in touch with the manager long in advance of the show to develop leads.

It is wiser to use such skills than to envision great fortunes to be made from hobby collections. Before sinking capital into collectibles, remember that a diamond, painting, or antique farm tool is worth only as much as someone is willing to pay for it, and the market is not always there.

But if you are a collector, you can make a profit by buying and selling wisely. A recent survey showed that, in a 10-year period, jewelry and diamonds increased in value by 100 to 400 percent; antique and classic automobiles by 200 to 400 percent, and postage stamps by an average of 250 percent.

A Tiffany art glass shade that originally sold for about $800 at the turn of the century, brought $74,000 at a recent sale. A five-line bill written by Paul Revere after the Boston Tea Party sold for $70,000 at an auction, and a first-year Superman Action Comic was worth nearly $5,000 to an avid collector.

A Missouri truck stop operator attended an antiques auction where an old clock caught his eye. He took it home, got it in running order and developed a new interest in horology as a result. He became skilled in clock repair and created a lucrative business for himself.

A Missouri woman who retired from her home economics teaching position makes wedding and birthday cakes. She enlisted the aid of her daughter, an artist, to design unusual decorations that set her cakes apart from commercial bakery goods and permit her to charge a hefty sum for their personalized products.

A Kansas woman who had worked for years in the kitchen of a children's home opened a small restaurant with special attention to menus for children. Because her place is strategically located at a busy highway crossroads, she attracts many tourist families.

However, if you are thinking of going into business for yourself, walk slowly and take short, careful steps. Pitfalls lie ahead and the road will not be smooth.

First of all, know your product, the market, the opportunities for growth, the chances of failure. According to the U.S. Department of Commerce, quoted by Morton Yarmon in the magazine, **50Plus**, October, 1981, growth areas in the preceding five years included real estate (455 percent gain); educational products and services (137 percent gain); printing and copying (137 percent gain); employment services (69 percent gain); restaurants, all kinds (47 percent gain).

In the same period, the biggest losers were listed as soft-drink bottlers, accounting, credit, collection agencies, general business services, gasoline service stations, laundry and dry cleaning, automotive products and services.

Yarmon suggested that those interested in franchise information get in touch with the National Franchising Association, Suite 1005, 1025 Connecticut Ave., Washington D.C. 20036.

But independent business ventures also may involve financial risk, if investors know too little or plunge too quickly.

A Vermont couple who had honeymooned in a charming, rustic hotel returned on a sentimental journey 25 years later and found it as attractive as they had remembered. Suddenly — even though neither had any merchandising experience — they were caught up in a longing to own and operate the hotel after the husband's retirement as a teacher.

For the next few years all they could think of was how they would redecorate and maintain the building, assuming they could persuade the owners to sell. They knew other couples would find it as lovely as they had.

Strangely, they discovered that the owners indeed would sell, and the Vermont man and his wife didn't question their good fortune. They made the deal and invested all their savings.

No one had told them the highway would be closed within three years. Obviously, the former owners had kept the secret well.

They struggled through the first two years but when the new highway was built, they hadn't enough capital to do extensive advertising that would have attracted new business.

Within months, they were broke, their dream destroyed.

The risks, of course, are not nearly as great if you know a business inside and out, as Carl Otto knew his special manufacturing field. One who is experienced in a given area of work knows the potential hurdles and headaches, how to spot trends, analyze the market and prepare for emergencies.

That's why Carl Otto and his son, Steve, also experienced in the industry, were able to take over a company and make it a growing and profitable concern. With the energy and enthusiasm of a much younger man, Carl Otto told an interviewer:

"Work keeps me healthy. I won't retire for a long, long time."

That's attitude, one of the four big "A's."

It was a drastic change in attitude that saved for the world the genius of "Bucky" Fuller.

The inventor of the geodesic dome and one of the age's most revolutionary thinkers felt that he was "really such a failure" as a young man that he actually thought of drowning himself in Lake Michigan.

Suddenly, he decided he had no "right" to take his life.

"I said to myself," he recounted years later in an interview, "that if I'm doing what the Almighty wants done to make humans a success, I won't have to go out and earn a living.... If I'm really doing what the Almighty wants done, I'll get on."

So can you.

Chapter 8
It's Back-to-School Time

The white-haired man walked with a cane, but his chubby face wore a Santa Claus smile as he returned the cheery greetings of the teenagers passing on the campus walk. At his side was a slim, vital woman whose gray, groomed hair contrasted with the brilliant blue of her pants suit.

"This has got to be the greatest thing that ever happened to me," he said. "Here I am going back to school, 10 years after quitting work, and these kids are my friends. I tell you, I feel 30 years younger."

He pulled a letter out of his briefcase.

"Look at this. I just sold my first short story and the editor wants to see more of my work. I've got to get home and write."

"And I have to study my lines," the woman said. "I've just been handed my first stage role."

This man was on his way from a creative writing class at the community college. The woman had been spending the morning in Senior Theatre. They are only two of the growing number of men and women who returned to school in an educational revolution that in recent years has swept the country, changing the lives of retirees everywhere.

Too many of their peers, however, are standing on the sidelines. For them, life still is a set-in-stone time span made up of the "three L's" — learning, labor, and leisure, and in that order. The first 20 or so years to be spent in the classroom; the next 40 or 50 on the job, and the rest sitting around doing nothing.

Of course, the game plan doesn't always

work, even for those who believe in it. Many a college student, still in the "learning" age category, also has an outside job. And many a wife has discovered that she doesn't automatically retire from housework and step over the invisible boundary line from the "labor" segment of life into that beautiful world called "leisure," just because her husband retires from his job. The dust, the dishes, and the dirty clothes don't disappear as if by magic the day after the retirement party.

A few enlightened managements and unions have encouraged midage schooling for employees, even arranging for sabbaticals from work. The four-day work week is designed in part to allow a blending of labor and leisure.

This is all to the good. We thrive on a balanced diet in all areas of life, not just at the dinner table. We can add zest and flavor and variety to every day by dividing the three units of learning, labor, and leisure into smaller slices, allowing time and opportunity for study, work, and recreation throughout life. Even kindergartners and great-grandparents can handle some of the household chores.

If you are one who believes in that three-unit time span, if you "finished" your education at 20 or 25 and throughout your busy career had no time to develop outside interests, you already have two black marks on your record. Don't make the third big mistake of sitting down the rest of your life because you feel that with all that learning and labor you have "earned" a few years of leisure.

To wake up in the morning with nothing to do all day may sound like heaven when you are 40. But when you're 70, it is self-imposed torture, cruel and inhumane self-punishment. Bones can ache and muscles can atrophy without activity. A mind can rust from lack of use. A heart can harden and hands can stiffen when they don't reach out to help someone. The sweetness of time can be cloying. Even a chocoholic can get a stomach ache in a candy store.

So how do you add some learning and some labor to this leisure life of retirement? In other chapters, you will read about part-time jobs and volunteer work. This chapter is for the new breed of classroom student, the silver-haired scholar.

Decide, first of all, what you want to do, what skill you want to develop.

Do you want to write and, perhaps, sell a story to a magazine? Are you working on your first novel or a nostalgic piece? Do you know how to research material, organize a story, or find a publisher? Creative writing classes are offered in every major city or by correspondence.

Do you want to act? Senior Theatre is springing up all over America. Students take part in drama workshops, put on plays, even public performances.

Do you want to know how to dance, how to fish, how to decorate a house or refinish a chair? Do you want to study the history of the Holy Roman Empire? Ozark folklore? the underground railroad? letters in the New Testament? television production?

Do you want to learn to paint a landscape, write a song, build a computer, play the piano, beef up your retirement income and slim down your taxes, gaze at the stars, or go adventuring in the mountain wilderness or the sun-drenched desert?

Just place your order. Like some fairy godmother with a piece of chalk for a magic wand, the schools of America will bring it to you on a platinum platter. Don't just sit there, longing for a more exciting life. You can create it for yourself.

When she was 87, Rose Brasch earned the bachelor's degree she had started 70 years earlier. She had dropped out of college to marry and rear a family but 11 years after she was widowed, the St. Louis grandmother decided to go back.

"I believe that when you start something you should finish it," she told a reporter on commencement day at the University of Missouri-St. Louis. "I always tell people, 'Don't ever get old. Stay young all your life.'

"Of course," she added with a chuckle, "when they ask me how to do that I say I don't know."

But Rose was determined to keep her mind active and to achieve a significant milestone.

Such a formal academic program may not be to your taste. On the other hand, if you didn't finish high school, you may want to go back for your diploma. Then you can go to college or take special enrichment courses after that.

Here are a few of the opportunities waiting for you.

General Educational Development

This a standardized nationwide exam administered by the American Council of Education in Washington, D.C. Originally intended for members of the military who dropped out of high school, eligibility for G.E.D. testing has been expanded. For information, get in touch with your Board of Education or the Continuing Education program at your nearest college or university.

Campus Courses

You can enroll for either credit or noncredit courses in an amazing range of subjects. Many schools offer a sizable tuition discount to those over 60. Whether you want a degree or just want to study again, whether you want to finish an interrupted academic program and begin a new one, check into the myriad opportunities in your area. While daytime classes may cost more, they appeal to many older students who prefer not to go out in the evening when most noncredit classes are scheduled.

Independent Study

Through correspondence courses, millions of Americans have learned school credits without leaving home or have taken special non-credit enrichment programs. That once-revolutionary idea has evolved into modern radio and television lectures and classes and off-campus study projects tailored to the individual's unique interests and educational requirements.

On an independent study program, you usually are permitted to travel at your own pace, but with faculty supervision. If you're working toward a degree, however, more stringent requirements may apply. Some schools require that out-of-town students spend a week or so of each semester on the campus.

If you are living in a retirement or nursing home, ask the activities director about the possibility of inviting a university spokesman to discuss setting up a class where you are and inviting other residents to take part.

The University of Missouri's Center for Independent Study offers more than 125 credit courses by correspondence. Enrollment is open the year round. Write the Center, 514 South Elm St., Columbia, Mo. 65211, for a catalog and information.

The University of Mid-America, a consortium of 11 schools, including The University of Missouri, administers a nontraditional study program. Through the use of television, cassettes, study guides, and other printed materials, this program provides an exciting alternative to campus-based classes. Information is available from your nearest University of Missouri/UMA office or from UMA, 429 Clark Hall, Columbia, Mo. 65211.

Elderhostel

This is for seniors who think young, for retirees with a lively interest in the world around them. None others need apply.

Elderhostel is one of the most exciting innovations in the field of adult education. Begun in the mid-1970s as a summer study and enrichment program for older Americans, it now operates on more than 300 campuses in most of the 50 states. It takes you either across town to a nearby university or across the country to study two or three subjects during your weeklong stay.

If you go out of town, you probably would be housed in a campus dormitory with 30 or 40 other seniors with a single goal: to learn. It is designed both for scholarship and friendship.

Each school offers a unique curriculum. You would make your choice of schools depending on your special interests and, of course, your financial and physical ability to travel to a particular campus.

For example, in the St. Louis area, Fontbonne College has offered such a mixed bag as "Music Since Edison," "The Amerindian and the Environment," and "Contemporary Moral Issues." At the University of Missouri-St. Louis, students from across town or across the country have studied "Television Production," "The History of Work in the United States," and "From Hunter-Gatherers to Nation States," with a tour of the largest prehistoric community in North America.

The variety is almost endless. For information on the Elderhostel program, get in touch with the University of Missouri-St. Louis, with Fontbonne College in St. Louis, or with Elderhostel, 100 Boyston St., Suite 200, Boston, Mass. 02116.

Bible Study

Of all the courses of study open to retirees, none is more helpful or inspiring or stimulating that a study of the Bible.

Now that they are free of the pressures of full-time work, many — even those who have never been serious Bible students — are devoting a portion of their time to a systematic study of the Scriptures.

Don't let it be burdensome. Let it be a joy. You may want to assign yourself a chapter or so every day, or a book every week. You may want to concentrate your study on the gospels, the prophets of the Old Testament, the Ten Commandments, or the parables of Jesus.

Whatever your "curriculum," it will be an enriching program and one to be shared. Your church may offer opportunities for Bible discussions through adult Sunday school classes or missionary societies. But, in addition, why not organize "cottage" meetings in your own home or on a rotating schedule, for some weekday afternoon? Together, you can plan a Bible study program that will be truly exciting as you explore the deeper meanings of this Holy Book.

Ask church friends to join, but don't be discouraged if only a few respond. Remember the words of Jesus (Matthew 18:20): "Where two or three are gathered together in My name, there am I in the midst of them."

The American Association of Retired Persons (AARP) and the National Retired Teachers Association have many enrichment programs.

Your public library, your church, a civic or service club in your area also may offer special courses.

The opportunities are everywhere in abundance. It's as though you had been handed a blank check for shopping in a supermarket. Would you stand outside, say you weren't hungry, and wouldn't bother to go in?

If you go in, how will you choose from this wonderful assortment? Will you grab everything you see? It's wiser to be selective. Even with a blank check, you should make out a shopping list in advance.

Attitudes and work plans are as important as one's purse and available time.

Ask yourself:

1. Do I **really** want to learn? What subjects?

2. Why? What is my goal? Do I want to (1) prepare for a retirement job? (2) develop a lucrative hobby? (3) delve into facets of my career field I never had time for before? (4) Do I just want to keep my mind and my body active (and that may be the most important reason of all) regardless of what I study?

3. Am I being practical? Will the hobby I'm counting on to bring in income mean more work (and fun) than profit? If I have never written before, can I reasonably hope to become a famous novelist or will I be content to learn the basics and start with simple articles and stories?

4. Are the course requirements, such as long field trips, within the boundaries of my own physical condition?

5. Will I try to overcome any sense of inadequacy or embarrassment among younger

students and accept them — and be accepted — as friends?

6. Do I have the persistence to keep going? Will I try hard to resist the temptation to be a dropout, especially if it seems a little tough at first? Will I be willing to put off a fishing trip to attend class or turn off a televised game if that's the **only** time I can study?

7. Can I work out a schedule that will permit me to enjoy that televised game, for example, or that fishing trip as well as my school work? Can I strike a good balance?

8. Can I attend classes and maintain a study schedule without inconveniencing others in the household?

9. Can I set aside a study nook where I won't be disturbed? Will I try to develop good study habits and keep a certain block of time available just for reading and work, letting nothing short of a household emergency interfere?

10. Do the other members of the household understand and accept my desire to do this and will they cooperate by not demanding that I give up my study time or work nook? By the same token, do I understand that they (and the house) also need attention and will I be amenable to their requirements?

If you have answered these questions to your own satisfaction, then you're ready to hit the books again. You'll find enrichment and adventure you never dreamed of as you face new frontiers of knowledge.

It's a wide, wondrous, and wonderful world. At this very moment, it's waiting for you.

"Thank God," wrote James Russell Lowell, "when you get up in the morning that you have something to do."

Chapter 9

Shut In But Not Shut Out

Giving up is the ultimate tragedy.

Robert J. Donovan, quoted in **Peter's Quotations: Ideas for Our Time** by Lawrence Peter, (William Morrow & Inc. N.Y., 1977)

Life's front door and back door and even the side door may be locked, but you can always open a window.

Home-based need not mean home-bound. Your body may not be able to travel, but your mind, like Superman, can leap over walls in a single bounce, and your heart can wander all over the world.

Even if you can't get out of the house, if you have no car or someone to drive you, or if you're in a retirement or nursing home, don't shift gears into reverse and back away from all the fun, excitement, adventure, and independence that are waiting for you.

They're not only in the world beyond your door, not only in the bustling universe outside your closed window. They are right where you are, this moment, even as you read these words.

Within the limits of your physical condition and your financial means—although you need not spend a great deal of strength or money in your search for adventure—you can do anything you want to do. You may not do it as skillfully, as quickly, or as easily as someone else, but that's not the idea.

The idea is to dream and to dare and to DO. Don't stumble down a gloomy path of inactivity and pessimism. Take the high road to adventure. Don't just wait out the days. Brush them with excitement and clothe them with joy.

Don't just survive. Don't simply exist.

Live!

You are a special person and you occupy a special niche that no one else in all the world can fill. You are a child of God, loved and cherished by Him.

If you cling to that thought, you will refuse to let your life frazzle out with a whimper like a wet firecracker, and you can live your days with a bang and with the glory of a skyrocket.

Write your own bill of rights, your own Declaration of Independence. Fate may have dealt you some rough blows. Who says you have to accept them?

"Independence," wrote Victoria Conley in **Rehabilitation Gazette,** "is an attitude."

Then the young disabled Chicagoan, associated with Access Living, an independent living agency, added a challenge.

"What creative things can you do?" she asked. "What adventurous things can you do?"

While she was speaking primarily to those in nursing homes, it's a challenge to every senior.

"This is where your problem-solving skills come through. There are many things to consider: where to go, how to get there, getting permission and cooperation from the nursing home, gathering all your strength and spirit to effectively deal with all the people along the way to get what you want. Should you succeed in your goal, you will have changed your attitude, your whole being. All the sides of you that it took to get what you wanted will have been strengthened. You will have used your creativity, your humor, your adventurous risk-taking side, your ability to relate to others to attain your goal.

"Living is growing and changing, and positive growing and changing brings about an attitude of independence. It is within everyone to develop, and it is especially important for people with disabilities to realize this potential."

An attractive St. Louis woman, Bettye Bielfeldt, did realize this and refused to be daunted by tragedy, the devastating blow of rheumatoid arthritis, which imprisoned her in a wheelchair. An active, exuberant 32-year-old businesswoman when she became ill, she has now spent one-half of her life as a near-helpless invalid.

But though her body is crippled, her mind and her heart and her spirit are lively and strong. She will not be shut away from the world.

"It was very hard to accept at first," she said. "In fact, it was shattering. But you do have a choice. You can either do the best with what you have and stop moaning and groaning, or you can drown in self-pity."

Although dependent on the loving care of a relative or attendant to care for her day and night, she found she could hold a pencil and, with special telephone equipment, developed a magazine subscription service in her home.

Despite the body blow that would have destroyed a less doughty spirit, she never lost her inner joy and her concern for others. "So many have greater difficulties than I have," she said.

As a member of the Commission for the Handicapped for the Catholic Church, she founded and became executive secretary of The Retreat for Shut-ins, which since 1960 has sponsored retreats for the disabled, chronically ill and elderly.

"We give them help — and a lot of love," she said.

For herself and others who are disabled, she developed this philosophy to help over the rough places:

"You can never limit your horizons."

A Missouri quadriplegic, disabled in an automobile accident, would certainly agree. Determined to create opportunities for independent living for himself and others, he founded a nonprofit organization dedicated to helping the disabled become productive citizens.

"Don't lock us away," he said to a newspaper reporter. "Let us establish our self-esteem. Let us earn our way."

This woman and this man have asked no quarter of life, only opportunities. Life managed to "retire" both of them long before they were old enough for Social Security. But the philosophy they share can inspire older men and women, whether in their own homes or in nursing or retirement homes, to refuse to be daunted.

Don't say you can't do anything. **Everyone** can do **something.** In other chapters of this book can be found opportunities and fun for retirees and suggestions for learning new skills and for creating exciting hobbies. If they aren't quite right for you, maybe the following will help.

1. Write the story of your childhood and of the town where you grew up. No one in the whole world can tell that exact story. Unless you put it down and save it, it will be lost forever.

2. Would others in the home where you live like to talk and write about their childhoods? Start a writing club. Send a nostalgic piece to a magazine. Such reference books as **Writer's Market,** available in the public library, will tell you what magazines would welcome such articles.

3. Start a little newspaper to report news about the residents—their hobbies, families, and life stories.

4. Are you a musician? Did you once teach piano or voice or perform in recitals? Get together with other musicians in the home to form an orchestra or glee club. Sing and play for your own amusement and joy, even if no one else wants to listen. Put on a little program. Sing the old songs and the hymns you love.

5. Are you a photographer? You need not be an expert to take snapshots. Start a little camera club. Put on a contest for the best snapshots. Ask the head of a nearby camera store or the photographer from a newspaper to work with you. Does anyone have a movie camera? Get together all the would-be actors. The writing club can develop a story and the camera club can film it. You can do this with only a small investment of money—and to "go Hollywood" could be one of the most exciting projects of your life.

6. Collect stamps. Even if you can't travel, you can go in imagination to the many countries represented on the stamps in your collection. Dig out the stories of those stamps, the legends and lore behind the portrait or picture, or specialize in certain stamps—kings or presidents or birds or ships or inventions or flowers.

7. Does the home where you live have a public address system for broadcasting announcements? Ask permission to put on little entertainment skits from time to time. Your acting and writing groups can make up some five-minute comedies or dramas as miniradio-shows.

8. This one will be more difficult, but others have done it and so can you. Become a ham radio operator. Talk all over the world.

A young Texan was almost totally disabled in an automobile accident when he was in his late teens. Give up? Not he.

Within a few years he not only obtained his amateur radio license but completed his college work and started on his doctorate in psychology. His bodily disability — plus his refusal to give up to this tragedy — then led him into a top post in the Institute for Rehabilitation and Research in Houston, Tex., where he could work for hundreds of thousands of other disabled.

His heart for adventure let him travel — both in body and in imagination — across the globe.

With the help of his wife and an attendant, he and his wheelchair visited many countries on behalf of the disabled. The places that he could not see personally he visited via ham radio, talking by shortwave to thousands of others who shared his hobby.

But, you say, you haven't the strength or the energy or the money to write or take a picture or start a club or buy hobby equipment.

So what can you do? For starters, you can express love. It doesn't take leg muscles or a strong back or a healthy bank account to smile. All it takes is a warm heart.

You can be a volunteer or you can be a friend, giving hours of your time or moments of your attention, telephoning or writing or talking to someone who needs you. And that someone, whether he or she is lonely or ill or troubled, **does** need you — right now.

On commercial radio and television there are many inspiring and helpful religious programs, free for the turn of a dial. You can hear a sermon, a report of religious happenings, discussions of issues important to every Christian. Without leaving home, you can participate in a worship service through the broadcast media. So keep your radio and TV schedules handy.

Even more important is to keep your Bible within reach. Turn to it daily for inspiration and comfort. The Lord's Prayer, in Matthew 6:9-13, provides our "daily bread" of spiritual sustenance. Psalm 91 gives us the assurance that "He shall give His angels charge over thee, to keep thee in all thy ways."

Magazines of meditations and books of devotion are available to meet our every need, to nourish our hearts and minds with a spiritual diet as essential to our well-being as the meat and potatoes on the dinner table.

Through giving and living to the utmost of your ability, you can make today, and every day, your own Fourth of July and proclaim your independence as a loving child of God.

No matter if the doors are closed and locked securely, fling open the windows and see the world.

Chapter 10
Political Action

This I do believe — that life has a real purpose — that God has assigned to each human a role in life — that each of us has a purposeful task — that our individual roles are all different but each of us has the same obligation to do the best he can.

Margaret Chase Smith and William C. Lewis, **Declaration of Conscience,** Doubleday & Co., Garden City, N.Y., 1972

Out of the American soil, nourished by the spirit of freedom and the tradition of revolution down through the decades, has sprung a grass-roots power — vocal, determined, and unstoppable.

It is senior power.

Product of a changing time, reflecting the turbulence that has turned old social and economic patterns topsy-turvy, it was founded and is supported by silver-haired, battle-scarred warriors who, in a nonviolent revolution, seek to topple the status quo in quest of "senior rights."

If you have not already enlisted, they need and welcome your support. Because of their pioneer work, seniors no longer need feel helpless when confronted by what they believe is mistreatment of the elderly. Join up. Move into the fray.

They're a daring bunch who will take on the high and the mighty and ask no quarter. Bunions, bifocals, bald pates, and all, these silver-tongued activists are on the march.

They comprise a grand and sometimes grizzled army of life's veterans, a debonair company of knights in creaking armor on the trail of the Grail. Fists figuratively clenched, they ache for a piece of the action. They're raiding the refrigerator of human rights, demanding a piece of the pie.

They've lost some battles but they've won many a skirmish. The Congress, 50 state legislatures, and thousands of state, county, and city officials have learned not to turn a deaf ear or put on their blinders.

Senior power speaks at the polls.

It hasn't been easy. The road leads uphill all the way, and it's studded with stones. In a cast of beefy heroes and beautiful heroines, senior citizens often are relegated to the role of spear carrier, far from the glare of the spotlight or the sound of applause. But in a world that worships youth, they are a special breed of battler, and they have the battle stars and scars to prove it.

Like a legion of little Davids, they aim their slingshots at a company of such Goliaths as horrendous health-care costs and big government red tape, inflation, high interest rates, probate laws and pensions, threats to social security and retirement benefits, condominium conversions that rob the poorer of their homes, and brutal crimes that kill or maim the weaker and lock them in a prison of fear.

At 76, the salty and peppery Maggie Kuhn was still one of the spunkier Davids. Founder of the 50,000-member Gray Panthers, a sometimes radical network of social activists, the former Philadelphia church worker became the high priestess of the senior set, as indomitable as a bulldozer.

The Gray Panthers headquarters is at 3700

Chestnut St., Philadelphia, Pa. 19104. Other major independent organizations working for senior rights include the American Association of Retired Persons, with special interest in health care costs, insurance, and work opportunities, 1225 Connecticut Ave. N.W., Washington D.C. 20036, and the National Council of Senior Citizens, 1511 K St. N.W., Washington D.C. 20005.

The Administration on Aging, a division of the Department of Health, Education, and Welfare, established under the Older Americans Act of 1965 and the Older Americans Comprehensive Services Amendments of 1973, is a clearinghouse for information on aging and makes grants to aid in the development of community programs and projects.

But America's seniors are not depending solely on the government for help. In fact, they have often battled with Washington. They are 20th-century crusaders, armed with statistics and marching on entrenched traditions and what they consider unfair treatment of older Americans and lack of protective legislation.

Even so, they are peaceful warriors, gentle rebels, on a mission of mercy for the old, the sick, and the lame. As He enunciated the Beatitudes in his Sermon on the Mount, Jesus might have been speaking of such as these.

"Blessed are the meek; for they shall inherit the earth . . . Blessed are the merciful; for they shall obtain mercy . . . Blessed are the peacemakers; for they shall be called the children of God" (Matthew 5:5-9).

These, indeed, are the meek, the merciful, and the peacemakers, joined in a cause they believe is right.

Their strength is growing with their numbers, and their voice, once a whisper, is heard in the land.

Magazines that cater to retirees spotlight seniors' activities and their quarrels with Uncle Sam.

In **50 plus,** published for "the fastest growing population" segment by Whitney Communications Corp., Washington correspondent Jack Anderson **(50 plus,** October, 1981, p. 63) called for a quadrennial White House Conference to replace the present once-in-a-decade schedule.

"The over-55 population . . . has increased over the past 20 years by 14 million Americans," Anderson wrote, "a 44 percent increase when the general population increased by 23 percent.

"In the next 20 years, the over-55s will increase by 19.4 percent because of better health care and general longevity. At the turn of the century, 21.2 percent of the population will be 55 and over.

"These numbers confirm the rapid mellowing of America. . . . I think every U.S. President should sponsor a White House Conference on Aging at least every four years. The issues revolving around older people are becoming too important to put on the shelf for a decade."

Politicians on the Potomac know this and recognize the voting power of this tremendous segment of the population. But that awareness is not limited to the Congress.

Many groups are tackling such problems at the state and local level. In St. Louis, a senior newspaper published job opportunities for older applicants eager to get back into the job market. In Missouri, the Silver-Haired Legislators have pushed for state protective services for the elderly. In Illinois, an indignant coalition lobbied for reductions in sales taxes on food and drugs.

"We don't want tokenism, like free deer licenses and passes to state parks," said Gerald J. Prete, president of the Illinois State Council

of Senior Citizens' Organizations. "We want meaningful economic legislation."

A spokesman for what has emerged as the strongest voice for seniors, the American Association of Retired Persons, has pointed to political action gains and challenged members to work for more.

In the Association's magazine, **Modern Maturity** (October-November, 1981, p. 4), Olaf A. Kaasa wrote:

"Among constructive actions that resulted during the 1960s, the United States Senate established a Special Committee on Aging, and the Social Security law was amended to increase minimum benefits, authorize early retirement at age 62, and provide coverage for an additional 160,000 older Americans. In addition, Congress passed the Older Americans Act creating the Administration on Aging as the chief provider and administrator of service programs for older people.

"It was not until the 1970s, however, that aging issues came to the forefront of national attention — in the press and on television, in legislative action, and in increased emphasis on the need for research in aging and better training in geriatric medicine. ...

"By late 1977, opposition to mandatory retirement had coalesced to such a degree that both houses of Congress passed legislation that made it illegal to force most workers into retirement before age 70."

But, Kaasa continued, "We must use our resources to see that the papers setting forth major recommendations do not gather dust."

Those recommendations, either at the national or state level, include increased transportation funding, nursing home reform, income tax relief, appropriations for in-home care of the elderly.

As a general in skirts, leading her troops into the fray, Maggie Kuhn has called for a "total revision" of the welfare system.

"Most of our social services system is highly paternalistic and obnoxious," she said. "What good does it do? The welfare system applies novocaine and Band-Aids. But the fact is people need jobs and housing and education."

Miss Kuhn, a retired church worker, took to the road in her older years and, like a gutsy circuit rider, preached the gospel of fair play for America's seniors.

At first, it was a lonely road.

Only five were with her when the idea of the Gray Panthers was conceived in a Philadelphia office. But those five — even as did the 12 who walked on the shores of Galilee 2,000 years ago — were destined to launch a gentle rebellion that would change the world.

To lead a revolution, no matter how free of violence and bombast and even physical danger, is not an easy task. To follow is not always comfortable. Followers, like their leaders, will hear jokes and jeers, face defeat, and sometimes walk with bleeding footsteps as they march over rocks of prejudice and stony tradition to establish a new frontier.

"But they that wait upon the Lord shall renew their strength; they shall mount up with wings as eagles; they shall run, and not be weary; they shall walk, and not faint" (Isaiah 40:31).

Chapter 11
Prayer

If God is for us, who can be against us? Certainly not God, who did not keep back His own Son, but offered Him for us all! He gave us His son — will He not also freely give us all things? Who will accuse God's chosen people? God Himself delcares them not guilty! Who, then, will condemn them?...Who, then, can separate us from the love of Christ?

Romans 8:31-35 TEV

We never stand so tall as when we are down on our knees.

We never are so strong as in the holy quiet of that hour when we acknowledge, without doubting, that the Source of all Power is outside ourselves.

Prayer is more than petition, for God knows our every need. Prayer is affirmation of God's government and constant care. Prayer is gratitude. Prayer is joy.

Prayer is constant communion with God and listening only to His voice.

Prayer is the hymn of praise sung by the psalmist. Prayer is the fidelity of Abraham, the struggle of Jacob at Peniel. Prayer is the sturdy faith of Moses, the unquenchable fire of Paul, the vision of John.

"Prayer," wrote James Montgomery, "is the soul's sincere desire, uttered or unexpressed, the motion of a hidden fire that trembles in the breast."

Jesus instructed His disciples:

"When thou prayest, enter into thy closet, and when thou hast shut thy door, pray to thy Father which is in secret; and thy Father which seeth in secret shall reward thee openly" (Matthew 6:6).

Here, in the "closet" of our own consciousness, that sweet, secret place deep in the heart where we hold fast our dreams, trembles the "hidden fire." No matter that wealth and success may sometimes dull the sharp edges of our need for spiritual sustenance — that flame burns with a steady light.

Our hunger for help from a Power higher than ourselves, in the turning of the human spirit to the Divine, can never really be filled. It is a part of man's being, the precious gift of God to His children.

And prayer does not go unheard or unanswered. Whether it takes the form of a magnificent anthem in the grandeur of a cathedral or a whispered cry in the solitude of a barren room, prayer lays its healing touch on the footsore and heartsick; it brings its promise to the trusting and its peace to the weary (Matthew 7:7-8).

So feed the hunger. Drink deep the draught. Your mental knees may creak from lack of use at the kneeling bench of your thought. The throat may be dry, and the words may tumble over one another in disorder. Never mind. God understands. His "hand is not shortened, that it cannot save; neither His ear heavy, that it cannot hear" (Isaiah 59:1).

Praise and affirmation may seem to be strangers in a world peopled by pain and haunted by the spector of loneliness. But even these cannot withstand the conquering power of prayer and the mustard seed of faith.

"The exercise of prayer, in those who habitually exert it," wrote William James in "The Energies of Men," "must be regarded by us doctors as the most adequate and normal of all the pacifiers of the mind and calmers of the nerves."

Can you give thanks in the midst of misfortune?

Of course.

Can you praise God in the darkness of life's night?

Yes.

Can you feel grateful when the dawn seems so far away?

Try. Just try.

Even though you cannot see the sun behind the clouds, it is there, in all its glory. Even though you cannot see the stars in a rain-swept sky, they are there, in all their beauty.

God's goodness never fails. It is man's feeble faith that falters (Matthew 21:21-22).

No one has fallen so deep into the dark pit of despair that he cannot see above him the first faint gleams of the morning light. No one has wandered so far into the wilderness of fear that he cannot glimpse, through the thickened roof of tree tops, the bright promise of the noontide.

When I survey the wondrous cross
On which the Prince of glory died,
My richest gain I count but loss
And pour contempt on all my pride.

(Isaac Watts)

As life's journey takes the new, unfamiliar, unmarked road of retirement — a road sometimes pocked with pain — we may be tempted to ask: "What have I to be grateful for?"

What, indeed?

The renowned minister and writer Norman Vincent Peale learned this lesson from his mother, who "taught her children, both by example and advice, 'You can do anything with yourself if you really want to.'"

In addition, he wrote in a column that appeared in the **St. Louis Globe-Democrat,** Aug. 6, 1981, she also warned her children:

"'To do that, you have got to keep in

tune with the highest. Never, never let yourself sag mentally. Cultivate a replenished spirit, and you can always meet life with victorious enthusiasm.'"

Her eminent son then added his own philosophical postscript:

"The Bible, which is always concerned with our welfare, also prescribes the uplifted spirit. It urges us to lift up our eyes unto the hills.

"So it is good to live with big things — mountains, music, art, big thoughts, great ideas — and supremely with God."

To pray to God for strength is the mark of the truly strong in spirit.

To pray to God for direction is the mark of the truly humble.

To give thanks to God in the grayness of the day is the mark of the truly grateful.

Moses prayed for guidance. Daniel prayed for deliverance. Jesus prayed that His enemies be forgiven.

Answered prayer was not for these alone. God still listens. God still cares (John 14:15-17).

In the midst of retirement joys and fears and adventure, let the "hidden fire" burn with a steady flame of gratitude and affirmation, petition and praise.

Let us pray not only in our distress, but also in the fullness of our joy; not only in the bleakness of want, but also in the abundance of God's blessings.

> **Lord of Glory, who has bought us,**
> **With Thy lifeblood as the price,**
> **Never grudging for the lost ones,**
> **That tremendous sacrifice;**
> **And with that hast freely given,**
> **Blessings countless as the sand**
> **[To all people in their labors]**
> **With Thine own unsparing hand.**
> **(Lutheran Worship 402)**